Lichfield

on old picture p

Roy Lewis

1. A favourite postcard view. This Raphael Tuck & Sons card shows the house where Samuel Johnson was born in 1709 and, facing it, the statue of Johnson by R.C. Lucas erected in 1838.

Designed and Published by
Reflections of a Bygone Age,
Keyworth, Nottingham

ISBN 0 946245 82 7

**Printed by
Adlard Print and Typesetting Services,
Ruddington, Notts.**

2. The north side of the Market Place as it was in 1905 before the statue of James Boswell was erected, with the shop of D.H. Williams, silk mercer and family draper, prominent on the right.

3. The Market Place about 1924 when it was the departure point for buses to Birmingham and Tamworth. On the right is the Victorian gothic of St. Mary's Church, rebuilt in 1870 as a memorial to Bishop Lonsdale whose son was vicar here. The Church now houses a Heritage Exhibition and Treasury of ceremonial silver.

INTRODUCTION

This book provides glimpses of Lichfield in the first fifty years of the present century as shown on picture postcards. Hundreds of postcards of the city were published both by national companies and by local photographers and stationers. However, most of the cards portray the same few places and scenes. Even local photographers, like W. Morrison in Bore Street and A.W. Mills in St. John's Street, and local printers, like A.C. Lomax's Successors (Lomax had retired in 1901), concentrated on the same scenes with very few postcards of lesser streets and local events. This has made it difficult to show many parts of Lichfield.

The selection reproduced here combines postcards showing popular attractions like the Cathedral, the Market Place with Johnson's House and Statue, and the old houses in Bore Street with cards showing streets rarely seen on postcards. A small number of private postcards showing people in Lichfield before the 1914-18 war has also been included.

The captions identify the place and add a few words about changes that have taken place since the card was published. Details are also given of the publisher, where known, and the date of publication. Most dates are best-guesses based on knowledge of the publisher, postmarks, and changes in the scene shown.

In compiling the book many people have offered information and advice. I gratefully acknowledge their help. They have made putting together the book a journey of discovery and pleasure. I hope readers will share this with me.

Roy Lewis
February 1994

Front cover:. Market Day in 1940 with traders' stalls in the Market Place and ladies resting beneath Johnson's statue.
Back cover (top): Lichfield Cathedral seen across Minster Pool photographed for Bradford publisher Walter Scott from the bridge in Bird Street.
(bottom): Bore Street in 1923 with Lichfield House on the left and the clock tower in the distance.

4. This bronze statue of James Boswell, Samuel Johnson's biographer, was given to the city by its sculptor, Percy FitzGerald. It was erected in the Market Place in 1908 when this photograph was taken.

Lichfield. Market Street

Valentines Series 50915

5. This postcard of Market Street looking towards the Market Place was one of a series published by Valentine & Sons of Dundee in 1905. On the right is the International Stores and, on the left, a man is looking into the window of Mrs Hackett, printer and stationer. The card was posted to Barrow-on-Soar in August 1909.

6. Market Street in 1923 seen from the opposite direction to the postcard above. Notice the large '26' over John Key's tailor's shop and the notice *"Motors for Hire"* beyond it.

7. Dam Street in 1935 with Hall's Old Curiosity Shop on the left and Sykes' China and Glass Shop on the right. The card was published by the Regal Art Publishing Co. of London.

8. The half-timbered building on the left of Quonians Lane was once Dame Oliver's School where Johnson learnt to read. Beyond it is the stonemason's yard begun by Robert Bridgeman, foreman stonemason at the Cathedral, in 1879. Postcard published by Judges of Hastings, and sent to Greenford, Middlesex, in September 1966.

9. Since the middle ages, the Cathedral has had a choir of vicars choral. This is the lower close or courtyard of their houses. Originally all the houses faced inwards on the yard but in the eighteenth century they were remodelled to face outwards. A Judges postcard of 1926.

10. The Upper Close of the Vicars Choral is approached through the entry on the right. These old houses are one of the city's hidden delights. Notice the potted plants outside the houses in this Judges postcard of 1926.

11. The Bishop's Palace, seen on this Walter Scott postcard, was built in 1687 to replace an older palace damaged beyond repair during the siege of the Close in the Civil War. Since 1954 it has been part of the Cathedral School.

LICHFIELD CATHEDRAL, WEST FRONT

12. An aerial view of the Cathedral and Close with the two Vicars' Closes in the centre foreground. Beyond the Cathedral, Stowe Pool and Minster Pool divide the Close from the old part of the city. An Aerofilms postcard of the late 1920s.

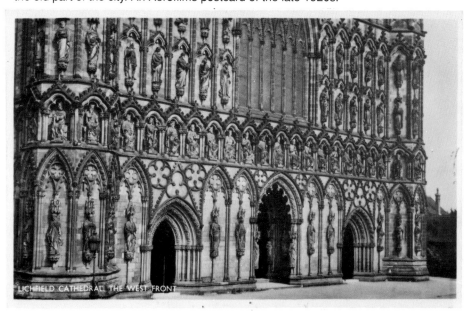

LICHFIELD CATHEDRAL. THE WEST FRONT

13. The west front is one of the glories of Lichfield Cathedral. The statues are nineteenth century replacements of medieval figures and show apostles, kings, saints and patriarchs, each identified by what he or she is holding. Card by Jarrold & Sons of Norwich.

14. This Walter Scott postcard of the west doors, the main entrance to the Cathedral, shows some of the statues in close up. They include St. Mary Magdalene, the Madonna and Child, St. John, and St. Peter.

The King leaving Lichfield Cathedral

15. This 1908 postcard of King Edward VII leaving the Cathedral is not what it seems. Edward VII never visited the Cathedral and the original photograph was taken in May 1894 when, as Prince of Wales, he was given a conducted tour by the Dean after visiting Lichfield to review the Staffordshire Yeomanry.

Lichfield Cathedral

16. The Cathedral choir is going from the South Choir Aisle into St. Peter's Chapel, then used as a vestry. The postcard is one of Raphael Tuck and Sons' *Oilettes* published about 1905 from a painting by Arthur Payne.

17. Ellen Jane Robinson died when her nightdress caught fire and a year later her younger sister, Marianne, also died. This monument, showing them asleep in each other's arms with Marianne holding a bunch of snowdrops, was carved by Sir Francis Chantry and erected in the Cathedral in 1817 by their mother, daughter of the Dean. This card was published about 1940 by Harvey Barton & Son of Bristol.

18. St. Stephen's Chapel in the Cathedral was restored in 1908 and a thanksgiving service held to mark the occasion. The postcard shows Bishop Legge (wearing glasses) preceded by his chaplain, Rev Cohn, with his pastoral staff, leaving after the service. The card was sent to Lincoln in July 1908.

-13-

19. A view of the Cathedral looking from the choir through the Victorian wrought metal screen to the west window. The choir stalls and Bishop's throne on the right were carved by George Evans – Seth Bede in his niece's novel Adam Bede. A Judges postcard of 1926.

20. Beacon Street looking north from the present day junction with Anson Avenue. The houses on the right were pulled down when the Little Barrow Hotel was built. A Valentine & Sons postcard of 1905, sent to Northampton in July 1908.

21. Beacon Street looking south in 1926. Beacon Gardens is on the left. This postcard was published by Mary Ferneyhough, who kept a shop and post office in Beacon Street.

22. In 1926 when Miss Mary Ferneyhough, postmistress in Beacon Street, commissioned this postcard, Beacon School was a residential school for children in need of special care.

23. A new Post Office for the city was opened in Bird Street in 1905 and E.T.W. Dennis & Sons of Scarborough published this postcard of the new building. The 'Swan Hotel' is on the right.

SWAN HOTEL, LICHFIELD, FROM THE BOWLING GREEN.

24. The 'Lilly White Swan Inn' was on this site in 1535. Long before this postcard was published about 1902, this had been shortened to the 'Swan Hotel'. The bowling green was opened in 1901.

25. The Lichfield Museum and Free Library, a building of yellow brick in an Italianate style, was opened in 1859. The Museum was moved out in 1958 and the Library in 1990.

26. The Prince of Wales Inn is on the right in this Beyond it is St. James' Hall, newly converted into th street.

ohic postcard of Bore Street in 1912 by A.W. Mills.
m' Cinema and advertising its attractions across the

27. Museums in the early part of this century were cluttered places, as shown by this view of Lichfield Museum in 1910 photographed by W. Morrison. It was said to contain *"fine examples of statuary, besides pictures, antiquities and local relics such as Johnson's shoe buckles."*

28. The public gardens near the Museum were also laid out in 1859. The fountain on the left was given by Chancellor Law in 1871 and the statue of Edward VII on the right by Robert Bridgeman when he was Sheriff in 1908. A Rotary Photographic Company postcard of 1912.

STATUE TO COMMANDER EDWARD JOHN SMITH, R.N.R.
RECREATION GROUNDS, LICHFIELD.

29. Commander E.J. Smith was captain of the ill-fated liner *Titanic* and went down with his ship. A national subscription raised money to pay for this memorial by Lady Scott, widow of the Polar explorer. Hanley, where Smith was born, refused the statue and it was then erected in the Museum Grounds at Lichfield. Postcard published by E.T.W. Dennis of London and Scarborough.

30. In July 1910 Dr. Baker allowed his children to have a day's "treat" in Lichfield with their Governess, Miss Sampson, and the nurse who looked after the younger boy. During the day this photograph was taken by local photographer W.A. Bullock.

31. The Garden of Remembrance by the side of Minster Pool was laid out in 1920 as a memorial to those who served in the 1914-18 war. This postcard was published by the Doncaster Roto Photo Co. in the following year.

32. Sandford Street looking towards Bird Street – another Valentine's series postcard of 1905. The photographer must have stood where the present day Swan Road crosses Sandford Street. The buildings in the foreground have been demolished and, on the left, one has had its top storey removed.

33. Bird Street in 1923 with the 'George Hotel' on the right and Sandford Street on the left.

Lichfield. Bird Street.

34. Bird Street looking north in 1907. The clock tower was once the Crucifix Conduit or public water supply. In 1863 it was given a new top and a clock. When the Friary road was constructed in 1926 all the buildings on the left were demolished. The tower was rebuilt on the round-about at the other end of the Friary road.

Old Houses, Bore Street, Lichfield.   Published by Lomax's Successors, Lichfield.

35. This 1905 postcard by A.C. Lomax's Successors shows a mixture of building styles. On the right is the sixteenth century Lichfield House (or Tudor Cafe), and beyond that Donegal House built in 1730, and the Victorian Guildhall.

43281. LICHFIELD: THE GEORGE HOTEL.

36. The 'George Hotel' is a fine late eighteenth-century building. Traditionally the headquarters of the Whig party, its postboys wore buff jackets (the party colour) and at election times Whig candidates addressed the people from the balcony. A Photochrom Co. Ltd. postcard of 1910.

37. The picturesque little shops under their seventeenth century gables, shown on this Boots postcard of Bore Street in 1934, were refurbished in 1967 and the shops are now set back under the upper storey.

Lichfield. *Conduit Street*

Valentines Series 51248

38. Conduit Street with the Corn Exchange, opened in 1850, on the left. When Valentine & Sons published this postcard in 1905, a butter and poultry market was held under the arches.

39. The Friary was an L-shaped house built on the site of the medieval Friary guesthouse. When the Friary road was built in 1926, the wing on the left was demolished and the rest incorporated in the Friary Girls High School.

40. The Old Man's Hospital, or St. John's without the Bars, was a medieval hospital refounded in 1495 as an almshouse for 13 poor and aged men. The tall chimneys to each room were added later. A postcard by F.W. Scarratt of Derby in 1915.

41. St. John's Street in 1922 with an early petrol pump on the left and the old Grammar School Headmaster's House, built in 1682, on the right. A Doncaster Rotophoto postcard.

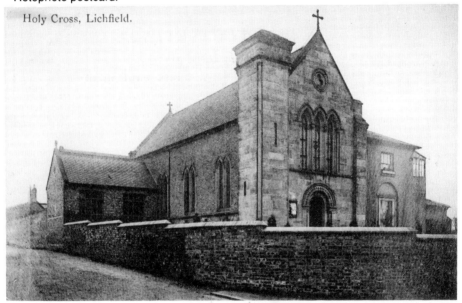

Holy Cross, Lichfield.

42. When Holy Cross Roman Catholic Chapel was built in 1803, it had a plain brick front so that it looked like a house and did not give offence in a Cathedral city. The stone front seen on this Marshall, Keene & Co. postcard was added in 1834.

King Edward VI Grammar School for Boys, Lichfield

43. King Edward VI Grammar School for Boys moved to this site on Borrowcop in 1903. In 1926, when this view was taken, the school had 120 boys, including 20 boarders.

King Edward Grammar School
Corner in Carpenters' Shop.

44. In 1926, woodwork was taught at the Grammar School in what an H.M.I. called *"a tumble-down hut made of unlined corrugated iron and extremely ill-lit by four small windows."* The hut was replaced in 1933.

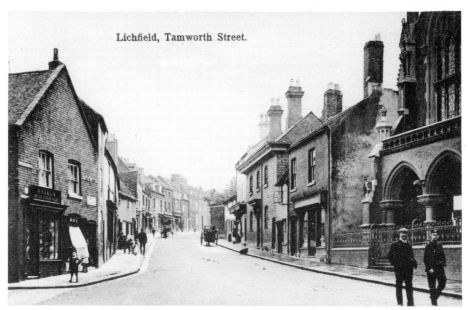

Lichfield, Tamworth Street.

45. This postcard shows Tamworth Street in 1907 with the Methodist Church on the right.

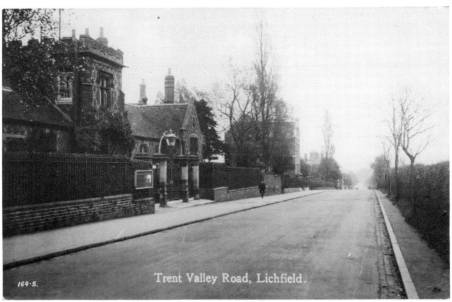

Trent Valley Road, Lichfield.

164-5.

46. This postcard, published in 1927 by W. Turner, newsagent in Tamworth Street, shows the entrance lodge to Lichfield workhouse built in 1840 in mock Tudor style and renamed St. Michael's Hospital exactly a hundred years later.

St Michael's Church, Lichfield.

47. St. Michael's Church is said to have been built on the site of a pagan shrine at the highest point on Greenhill. It was much restored in the nineteenth century. A 1910 Raphael Tuck & Sons' postcard.

48. St. Michael's huge churchyard was the burial ground for the city. Johnson's parents are buried here. On the right can be seen St. Michael's Schools. Another Raphael Tuck & Sons' postcard of 1905, posted some twelve years later to Bakewell.

49. A view of Greenhill in 1905, with the spire of St. Michael's Church in the distance and below it the drinking fountain and cattle trough put up in memory of Rev. J.J. Sergeantson, Rector of St. Michael's. A Valentine & Sons postcard, postally used in September 1906.

50. This postcard of St. Chad's Church was published by A.W. Mills in 1910. In the distance are the eighteenth century Stowe House and Stowe Hill, and in the foreground the thatched St. Chad's Well House.

51. Unfortunately we do not know the identity of this couple in their smart turn-out who posed in front of St. Chad's Church for this private postcard of 1910.

52. St. Chad is said to have stood and prayed in the spring here. The water was a remedy for sore eyes and in the 1830s a local doctor, James Rawson, built over the spring the stone structure seen on this 1915 postcard by F.W. Scarratt of Derby. It was taken down in the 1950's.

53. This postcard of St. Chad's Cottage was posted in 1907 by Agnes Smith, who lived in it, to a friend in New York. In the 1920s it was in the library of Berea College, Ohio. In the 1980s it was sold to an English postcard dealer visiting the United States and is now in my collection.

54. A view from the bottom of Leyfields looking south to Curborough Road and Dimbles Hill. In the distance is the Leyfields Post Office and Stores. This 1935 Regal Art Publishing Co. postcard is one of very few that show housing estates of the early 1930s.

55. The houses in St. Chad's Road shown on a card by the same publisher are decorated for George V's Silver Jubilee in 1935. Today the entrance to Netherstowe School is opposite them.

164-12.   St. Chad's Road, Wissage, Lichfield.

56. This rural scene is unrecognizable today. If you want to locate the spot, stand in Wissage Road near its junction with St. Chad's Road and line up the distant spires of the Cathedral. A 1927 postcard published by W. Turner, newsagent, of Lichfield.

The Locks Canal, Lichfield

57. This 1905 Valentine & Sons' postcard shows the Wyrley and Essington Canal not far from where it passed under St. John's Street.